A SHY

GUIDE TO

NETWORKING

A Practical Guide to

Networking For

Business Success

Melitta Campbell

To Brian: Thank you for your encouragement
and support over the years, especially during
my many wobble moments!

TABLE OF CONTENTS

FOREWORD

I first met Melitta more than a decade ago when she was active in the women's network inside Lloyds TSB. WIN held a corporate network group meeting there, which was a great success.

Networks can be incredibly helpful in accelerating growth, enthusiasm and creating a sense of belonging. They help each member feel nurtured and supported and from there, great things are possible.

In this book, Melitta shares her story of networking as a shy person and provides great insights into what she has observed, learned and practiced. She tells us what works and what doesn't and that victory is possible for everyone, no matter how you feel about networking today.

As she says, even a shy person can do this, so why not you? There are so many ways we can network - not only the way of the extravert. What the world wants is the genuine you, connecting with people with openness and authenticity. But we all benefit from a little help on the way. This is what Melitta gives you in this book, along with reassurance that you can do this, whether networking for your business or for a project you are working on.

With many people working from home and hierarchical structures crumbling, networking is more important today than ever.

Networking is not only about you. It is about finding a common ground with someone whose purpose matches yours. Together you will sparkle with joy because that meeting, that encounter, expands the world for both of you.

Thank you Melitta for writing this timely book.

Kristin Engvig
Founder, WIN &WIN Conference
WIN- Women's International Networking

INTRODUCTION

"This is your journey.

There is no right or wrong way,

only your way."

Melitta Campbell

As an introvert, who grew up feeling shy and awkward around strangers, networking was always a terrifying prospect. So, you can imagine how amused I am when I'm told that I look like such a natural networker, or when someone remarks, "I could never have your confidence". Little do they know that it's taken me close to two decades and a lot of hard work and courage to reach this stage. They have no idea that inside, I can still feel my inner shy girl desperately wanting to hide behind her Mum until it's finally time to go home.

I know that I'm far from alone in my battle with networking. And yes, it really did feel as terrifying as going into battle in the early days, and occasionally still does if I'm honest! But, I've learned just how powerful having a strong network is, and how enjoyable the experience can be. This knowledge helps me to push through any 'wobble moments' and come through the other side feeling happier and stronger and, ready for the next battle.

Over the years, my network has presented me with so many incredible opportunities and wonderful friendships that I never would have experienced if I had not learned the skills and taken the courage to push myself out there into the 'networksphere' time, after time, after time.

With this knowledge, I wanted to write this book to share how you too can overcome your fear of networking, and what I've learned works. However you feel about networking right now, and no matter how shy you believe yourself to be, you can become comfortable with it. And it is *so* worth the effort. You have so much to gain. Shy girls (and boys) CAN network - I promise!

In fact, as we go on this journey together, I'll show you the many ways in which your inherent traits as an introvert can actually be to your advantage when it comes to networking. I'll also share with you my secret hacks to getting around those moments when your doubts stand in the way of your good intentions, setting you free to enjoy a lifetime of new connections and opportunities. And, that's important because no one succeeds on their own.

We all need external perspectives, additional support or knowledge, fresh inspiration or encouragement from time to time. That's what your network will do for you. It's the ultimate shortcut to everything you want to achieve!

At every stage of this book, I want to you be mindful of two things. Firstly, that this is *your* journey, and secondly, there is no right or wrong way, only *your* way. If any of the ideas I suggest or steps I share don't feel right for you (yet!), then take a moment to think about what would. You don't ever want to be, or try to be, someone you're not.

It's when you show up as your 'real self' that you will feel most comfortable and be able to connect with others most powerfully. That said, you *do* want to grow into the best version of yourself, one that is capable of realising all of your goals and dreams. This takes growth – and growth takes courage. The good news is, I know you can do it, and I'm going to give you clear guidance every step of the way.

I've split this book into two parts. The first will go behind the scenes and help you prepare yourself for the journey ahead. To push outside your comfort zone is never easy. But, where willpower can fail us, a system can step in and help you continue moving forward. That's where my VICTORY

Formula comes in. I'll show you how to use this formula to build a foundation for success based on a clear vision and growing confidence. It will keep you getting 'out there' … even when every fibre of your being just wants to curl up safe at home with a mug of hot chocolate and a good book.

In the second part of this guide, we will dive into the 'networksphere' and see how it all comes together. I've split this section into three subsections: pre-event, in-event and post-event. As soon as I mastered what to do before and after an event, I found I became far less stressed at the event itself and I started to enjoy amazing outcomes and new opportunities. It was a game-changer! But, from talking to and training people in how to network successfully, I've discovered that (like my old-self) most people do not pay much attention to the pre- and post-event stages. Instead, they put a lot of pressure on themselves to turn up and say the right things, meet the right people and, distribute all their cards and brochures during the event itself. This is not only daunting and exhausting, it's not very effective either. I'm going to show you a better way – one that you can take at your own pace and enjoy!

So, that's what lies ahead. But, there is one last thing to prepare before we go any further. If your goal is to improve your networking skills, then it will be important to not just read this book and nod along, but to use it as your action guide. I recommend that you buy a new notebook to accompany you on this journey. Or, if you're like me, use one of the many beautiful notebooks you have stacked at the back of your stationery cupboard just waiting for the right occasion to be used … this is that occasion! Use your chosen book to note down your answers to the questions I ask, record your ideas

to the spot as if my shoes were made of concrete, as I pushed myself to walk forward into the throng of happily conversing people. I have never been good at small talk and I was forever getting tongue-tied. I don't know if it was my shyness or the fact that I grew up with two different accents and every so often would get caught between them, but sometimes my words just came out garbled. Each time this happened, it caused people to lean in and look confused. That made me feel all the more awkward! It felt like I had all these words and phrases whirling around in my mind, but I just couldn't get hold of them in any eloquent order. So, my words came out mumbled and my cheeks would flush with embarrassment. I would long for the day that they would invent blush-proof make-up! My panic would trigger the 'little voice in my head' which would dutifully go into overdrive. 'You don't belong here. Everyone is wondering why you came. Why would anyone listen to you? You're boring! You have nothing valuable to share'.

I frequently looked in awe at people who could strut confidently around a room effortlessly engaging in conversation. I was convinced that would never be me.

Today, my stomach still clenches when I walk into a room of strangers ... but only momentarily. It finally dawned on me that no one else can see what I feel on the inside. When I feel overwhelmed by an event I breathe deeply or, even take a short break to recharge before getting back to making new acquaintances. Did you know it's OK to do that?! It's been quite a journey but now I am (mostly) comfortable with feeling uncomfortable. In this section, you'll learn how you can do the same.

While you may be tempted to skip straight to the second part of this book, I would encourage you to start here first. It won't take you long to get through it. But, the seven-part VICTORY Formula you'll create will give you the understanding, perspectives and drive needed to implement the tools in the second section. Without this formula, you'll find it much harder to push outside your comfort zone and network with ease. The bonus part is that the VICTORY Formula will likely help you with many of your other goals in life that you have been holding back from too!

The Formula includes:

Vision, **I**ntention, **C**ourage, **T**rue-self, **O**bstacles, **R**ules and reminds you that **Yes! Y**ou've got this!

Vision: setting out your future networking success

Your vision gives you an awareness of where your hard work and commitment is taking you. It brings your future success and what that looks and feels like for you into the present so it feels more tangible. This also makes it easier for you to stay focused and motivated. Looking into your future might sound a bit 'woo woo' or a strange place to start, but it will make a big difference. In those moments when taking a particular action feels hard, having clarity about the outcome you are working towards will help you to take that step. The bigger your vision, the smaller the obstacles that stand between you and success will seem.

I suspect you already have a vision. It might not be as clear as it needs to be, but if you didn't have a desire for a future that's different from today, you wouldn't have opened this book. So, let's start there. Why *did* you open this book and start to read it? While networking may not be a fun activity for you right now, some part of you is aware that you want (or need) to improve. Your task now is to transform that awareness into a clear vision.

Have you ever faced a tough challenge before? I don't mean something like climbing Kilimanjaro (though it could be!). I'm more referring to a time when you dared to tackle something that you were not convinced you could do. When you face these challenges, they will fall into two camps. One will be those things you feel you can't do, but know you want to. And, those you feel you can't do and you're not really bothered about succeeding in. Which do you think you will have more success with?

Understanding that the hard task ahead of you is something that you *want* to achieve is key. It gives you the determination to stick with it. It's that motivation and grit that will help you master networking, because mastering anything takes time and commitment. This first requires that you have an interest or passion in it. This is where your vision comes in.

I remember the first time I went into town shopping on my own. I was seventeen. I got myself ready, made sure I had the right coins for the bus and left the house. I felt a bit nervous but not enough to stop me. My goal was to get some ideas for Christmas presents before deciding what to buy and for whom. I walked to the bus stop and boarded the right bus (there was only one, so that part was easy). I arrived in town and made my way to the first shop I wanted to browse. I went inside. It was a busy Saturday and there were people everywhere. It was hard to see what was on the shelves because of the number of people in the way. I felt my cheeks prickle with heat and my chest tighten. I felt so out of place and overwhelmed. All I wanted to do at that point was go home.

So I did. I lasted less than 20 minutes. Mission most definitely not accomplished.

Two years later when I went to university, knowing how shy I could be, my mother suggested that I opt for a double room so I would have some company. However, when I arrived at my university Halls in the early autumn, I found myself alone in my room. An hour later it was confirmed … my roommate wasn't coming. I had already unpacked my things by this point and sat on my bed wondering what to do next. I fiddled about tuning in my TV, then sat back on the end of my creaky metal bed. Then it dawned on me. If I don't do something, I could be sat in this room on my own for the next three years! I may be shy, but I'm not a loner. I love having friends.

Earlier in the day, I had explored the Halls where I was staying with my Mum before she returned home. We found dozens of identical rooms and bland corridors. At the far end of the building we also found a large common room with ancient orange fabric sofas lining the walls. Recalling this, I sprang up off my bed. I decided to knock on some doors and invite people to a party in the common room that evening. So, with my heart in my mouth, I set about my mission before I had second thoughts. Every door I knocked on was opened by a warm smiling face, or two. It soon became apparent that I wasn't the only one feeling alone and unsure. I quickly grew in confidence as I continued from door to door. Many of those smiling faces joined me in sharing the invite with our mystery hall-mates (saving my sore knuckles!) and within an hour we'd invited everyone. Mission accomplished! And, I had made some friends straight off the bat!

When the party started, the only person everyone knew was me and so I by-passed that awkward introduction part. It was a great start to my new life and I was so pleased I had taken the initiative. It was also a technique I've used in my networking too.

On occasions when I felt particularly unsure and/or new to an event, I've volunteered to welcome guests or give out name badges. It's a great way to meet everyone early on and subsequently get welcomed into conversations later.

You may be asking, "What was the difference between your first outing into town and your first day at university, Melitta?" In a word, my answer would have to be 'vision'.

In the first instance, I didn't have a strong reason to stay in town once it felt uncomfortable. I could always go back another day with my Mum or with friends. But, when I was alone in my university room it was clear that if I didn't take the action I felt nervous about, I risked being alone for the duration of my studies. The fear of being alone was greater than the fear of meeting new people. That vision of having friends vs being alone gave me the motivation to move out of my comfort zone.

When creating your vision of the future, you want to ensure that your fear of not achieving it is greater than the fear of the steps you have to take to get there. The bigger and brighter your vision, the easier it will be to step over your fear of networking.

This brings me back to my first question. Why did you pick up and read this book?

Read the following questions, then answer them in your *Networking Success Journal*. If the answers aren't immediately clear to you, then journal around them. If you are new to journaling, the idea is very simple, but also very powerful. It requires you to write your thoughts down on paper. You want to do so without self-editing or judging your thoughts as you go. Just let your ideas flow. No one else needs to ever see your notes. They are just for you. Once finished, reflect on what you have written to see if you can identify any patterns or spot any hidden meaning, blocks or opportunities. It's a wonderfully liberating and insightful exercise.

Your vision shows you what life will be like once you have achieved your goal to become a more confident networker. Take your initial answer, the reason you opened this book, and then use the following questions to help you develop your vision further.

Imagine you are 12-months into the future and you have achieved your goal. How will you feel when you walk into a networking event? What is your posture like? What are you wearing? How do you greet the person at the welcome desk? Who do you meet as you move around the room? How do they react to you? How do you feel about that? What emotions do you experience when you leave at the end of the event? When reflecting on the conversations you had during the event, which encounters make you smile, why? Close your eyes and picture this in as much detail as you can. Add in colour, sound, smells, tastes and texture into your vision so it feels as real as possible. Imagine how someone's hand feels when you shake it, what the room smells like, how the wine tasted, how you feel at each interaction...

Having a clear networking vision gives you the sense of purpose needed to motivate you into action. This purpose will also give those actions, and your ultimate success, greater meaning and value.

Visit your vision every day to keep your goal front of mind. You can close your eyes and imagine watching your future-self networking confidently, as if watching yourself on a movie screen. Or, you can turn your vision into a board full of images that represents what achieving your goal means to you. Choose whichever option appeals most to you.

Do you remember the blank pages you left at the front of your notebook? I want you to go to them now and write your networking vision. You can add pictures, beautiful text, inspiring quotes, colour or other exciting elements for emphasis if it helps. Placing your vision at the front of your *Networking Success Journal* will serve as a frequent reminder of the journey you are on and why your efforts are worth it, keeping you focused and motivated.

Now you have your inspiring vision – let's add some intention!

Intention: Deciding what you want most
'Where attention goes, energy flows'. This is a phrase I have heard countless times during my years of professional, personal and mindset development. I have found it to be very true. And it applies to your commitment and desire to network effectively as an introvert.

How do you feel when you think about networking? If you feel anxious and you focus on that feeling, your anxiety becomes worse sometimes to the point where you become so fearful that you either feel paralysed or compelled to run in the opposite direction. This sense of being stuck or wanting to run away is your brain's way of protecting you.

In centuries gone by, when you felt fear it was usually because you were in serious danger. You might have been under threat of an attack from a sabre-tooth tiger or a hungry bear. In this instance, your brain's amygdala (the part of your brain that deals with emotions, fear and aggression - and still thinks you live in the jungle) would trigger your 'Fight, Flight or Freeze' instinct. This stress response would help you instantly take the appropriate action and live to enjoy another day.

We may have evolved significantly since our days in the wild, but our basic survival instincts remain with us. This is still important. If we were to feel no fear at all, we'd soon become reckless and put ourselves and others at risk. However, it is important to correctly assess our fears and emotions. Some fear responses hold us back from danger, some hold us back from our goals. It's up to us to make that distinction and act accordingly. For introverts, it's especially helpful to grasp truths.

Understanding this empowers us to manage our responses accordingly. As a 'shy girl', I've learned that when I start to feel fear, I need to breathe deeply. This reassures my brain that I am not under attack and allows it to relax. It sounds easy, and the beauty of this trick is - it is! Breathe out to empty your lungs, and then in slowly and deeply for the count of three. Then breathe out as slowly as you can for the count of six, releasing as much air as possible. This is the Emptying Breath technique. It activates your parasympathetic nervous system and quiets your sympathetic nervous system. In other words, it helps you to calm down. Do this three times and you will already feel much better.

Once calm again, you can focus on your intentions over your fears or doubts. To do this, of course, you first need to know what these are!

Before you can take that all important first step to complete an endeavour, you first have to *decide* that you are going to do it. This simple act of resolution will already rid you of many of your inner emotional conflicts. Decide that you *are* ready to do this, and then go for it. Looking back, that's what happened that first day in Halls. I decided that I needed to take action and knock on doors. That clear intention made it easier to follow through with the appropriate action.

Your intention builds on your vision by clarifying why achieving that vision is important for you. Do this by considering the following questions.

- What will you be able to achieve in life, in your career, or in your business once you can network with greater ease and success?
- Why is that important to you?
- What are the consequences if you *don't* have that?
- Does that worry you? Why? / Why not?

These insights confirm that the journey you're about to embark on is important to you. They've also shown you how and why. You have your starting point. You now know where you are today and what about that situation you want to be different. And, you have your vision of a better future. What follows in the next section will be the bridge between these two positions.

To help you make good on your intentions, let's get you some courage and confidence next!

Courage: Being brave and building confidence

Undertaking any new project or activity takes courage. Especially when it's something that you don't feel naturally inclined to do – like networking for most introverts. I want to encourage and congratulate you for making the decision to read this book, and following through on that intention! It demonstrates that you already have a level of commitment to improve your networking game, push your boundaries and experience more. That is a big advantage. I want you to take a moment to recognise this.

While reading this book may feel like a small thing to do, it's perhaps one of the most important decisions you could have taken. Too often, we allow ourselves to stay stuck in our comfort zone, when more often than not, the thing we desire is within touching distance. It's always easy to dream about how things could be different. But it takes courage to *make* them different. Often in taking those actions, we discover that it's easier than we first thought, and that we have more skills and abilities than we previously realised. This is when our confidence starts to grow.

I want you to take a moment to recognise the brave step you have just taken. Then note that in doing so, you have already gained a little bit more confidence. Seriously! Recognising and celebrating even the smallest steps you take along your journey to become a more confident networker will reinforce the progress you are making. It is that recognition that will help you build your courage and confidence one step at a time.

What's the difference between courage and confidence? As I see it, (please note that I am not a trained psychologist, so this is just my personal view), courage is equal to being brave; it's going out there into battle not knowing if you will survive or not, but feeling deep down that it's the right thing for you to do. Confidence is slightly different. It's the belief that no matter what happens during the battle, you can handle it; you can figure things out and come back in one piece.

You don't need to do or know anything in order to be brave and network, you just have to step up and go for it. However, to have confidence, you need to have some level of trust in your abilities. That means, each time you courageously get out there and network, you build a bit more confidence in your ability to do so. If you find that you have to be courageous all of the time, then you will come away an exhausted nervous wreck. Building confidence will help you to rely less and less on courage therefore enabling you to go out and network more and more. That said, confidence can deplete over time. If you don't use it, you lose it. Once built, you will need to find ways to keep your confidence alive by going to at least one networking event per month, for example, rather than one a year.

To put this into context, let me show you how this has worked for my daughter. When she learned how to ski, it took courage to strap two planks of wood (or whatever fancy materials they are made from today) to her boots, point them down the hill and slide. After doing that a couple of times however, she built up her confidence and bit by bit that confidence enabled her to keep going and build her skills. Having taken a break from skiing over the last two years however, fear has started to creep in and now she's having to start all over again. Her skills are no doubt still there, she's just lost faith in them. This time around her confidence will probably grow quicker, but she still has to go through the process of building it. Your networking confidence will be the same, so when setting yourself goals, be sure it includes attending networking events regularly.

Your courage will come from your vision and intention, accompanied by some deep breaths where required. Your confidence will come from your preparations, covered in section 2, and will build with your ongoing networking practice. That said, it's unlikely that you are starting from ground zero in your journey. Kickstart your confidence by noting down the experiences and existing resources you have access to today, which can support your networking efforts.

For example, what networking experiences have gone well for you, and what did you learn from them? This knowledge is a resource that's available to you. This book is also a resource. Which quality networking events do you have access to? Who do you have around you who can support you? Brainstorm everything you already have at your disposal and write these in your *Networking Success Journal*.

I want to take a moment here to highlight something important. Learning a new skill isn't about speed, it's about mastery. And mastery, takes time and passion. There's no race here. No expectation or pressure. There's just you deciding to take matters into your own hands and work towards a goal that you want to achieve - your vision of a better future. Avoid the temptation to judge yourself or compare your journey or outcomes to those of others. Instead, give yourself the permission to go at your own pace, and celebrate every step of your progress. I always like to remind myself that, 'Slow is smooth, and smooth is fast'. Feel free to add that to your *Networking Success Journal* if it resonates with you.

True: Becoming and loving your best self

It's hard to be confident when you don't know who you are. That was much of my problem in my early days of networking. I didn't really know who I was in terms of what I stood for, what was important to me or what my unique value was. Being blind to these caused me feel anxious and out of place. Once I took the time to explore these aspects of my character and beliefs, things started to shift. I made better connections, found exciting new opportunities and was able to add value to conversations with confidence. This part of the formula will help you do the same by bringing your true self to the surface.

The first thing that's important to understand are your **values**. Once you can make choices that are in alignment with your values, identity and purpose, you'll find them much more impactful. You'll create greater resonance and both you and those around you will feel the difference. Once you're showing up as your true self, you'll also feel more confident and less like an imposter. Sound good?

Take some time now to think about what your values are. You may find that your personal values differ from your professional ones. That's OK. You can create two lists if you find that most relevant for you. You may find it helpful to Google 'List of Common Values' to inspire you. Then follow this process:

- Determine your top 10 values
- Put this list in order, with the value that's most important to you at the top.
- Finally, highlight your top three and write them in your *Networking Success Journal*.

If you are finding it difficult to identify your values, think about what you admire or abhor in others. Who do you most enjoy spending time with? What makes you feel that time with them is well spent? How would you like people to feel about you after they've met you? Questions like these can provide helpful clues as to what traits you feel are most important to have and display. Be prepared to spend some time on this exercise, especially if it's the first time you've considered your values. It can be extremely hard to narrow your focus around what is most important to you. Take the time you need.

When I did this exercise for the first time, I looked at what was the most important to me on a personal level: thoughtfulness, attention and openness. I then considered what was most important to me in my role at the time as Head of Communication: consideration, openness, and connection.

You can see there are some clear overlaps between the two, with slight differences to account for the different ways I needed to show up for others. Once I became clear about my values, I was able to behave in accordance with them, and make stronger decisions and judgements. This instantly made me feel more confident and helped me build my credibility faster. It also made it easier for me to be myself when networking. Once I was able to show up as my true self, I saw a positive change in the way people reacted to me. Knowing who I was didn't just give me confidence, it gave others confidence in me too.

The next part of you to explore is what makes you special. What's your **zone of genius**? Once you know this, you can bring it out in your networking conversations so your contributions stand out as valuable and memorable, and your conversations feel more natural and authentic.

You want to find two or three things that you excel at. Finding your zone of genius can be challenging. You may be one of the lucky ones whose talents have always been clear to them. But, if you are like most people, your genius skills feel so natural that you might not have registered them as outstanding, or as being things that not everyone can do with your excellence, passion or joy. If you fall into this latter category, it can be helpful to ask others for their insights. Reach out to a few people who know you well and that you trust and ask them: 'In your experience, what is something you feel I do extremely well, perhaps better than others, that you've realised that I haven't noticed for myself?' You'll be amazed and touched by the responses you get. It will help you see how others perceive and value you. And, this will help you to see and start valuing all that is amazing about you too.

Once you know your values and unique talents, you also want to recognise that *you* are important to you too. Taking time for **self-care** might not appear to have an obvious connection to networking but, to my mind, it has *everything* to do with it.

Your ability to make success happen requires you to have respect for yourself and believe that you deserve a better future. When you engage in regular self-care practices, you reinforce the idea that you *are* worthy. I've incorporated into my daily planning a section I call: Mind, Body and Soul. Every day it prompts me to take at least 15-minutes for my personal development (mind), to be mindful of my healthy habits (body) and to engage in an activity that's only purpose is to bring me joy (soul).

Added to my practice of gratitude (taking a couple of minutes a day to acknowledge some of the highlights of my day), these self-care activities help keep my energy and positivity levels high, further fuelling my ability to perform at my best.

A nice side effect I've noticed in starting to develop belief and self-confidence is that I no longer compare myself to others.

Instead, I appreciate them for everything that they are, knowing that their brilliance does not reduce my own. I recognise that they are on their own journey, and I'm inspired by all they've achieved. This has been a huge win for me. Once I embraced what makes me different, including the imperfections along with the good, I started to enjoy a wonderful sense of self-ease, which has helped make my networking feel more graceful. I'm not sure if that's the right word to use, but as I used to feel so out of place and awkward, it's the best expression of the change I've experienced. I hope you start to enjoy the same too. Then you can tell me if I chose the right word or not.

I've come along way, but not without a fair number of wobble moments! These are inevitable, but not unsurmountable – at least not when you have your backup plan!

Obstacles: Creating your backup plan

Despite our best intentions, things don't always go according to plan. There will be times when your courage fails you, when something unexpected will cause you to stall, or when you start to feel "I can't do this". In these situations, your back-up plan will help you get yourself back on track quickly.

Take a moment to think ahead to your next networking event. Knowing your typical emotions and reactions, what is most likely to stand in the way of your good intentions? For example, what might discourage you from registering for an event or connecting with people the way you want to? What might cause you to feel anxious?

Take a blank page in your notebook and draw a line down the centre of a page from top to bottom. In the left column, write down all the different things that could trip you up or hold you back. Next, in the right column, think of an action you can take in each case to minimise the risk of each occurrence having a negative impact or holding you back.

I'm aware that this may sound counterintuitive, but action is the best antidote for fear. We are only ever fearful of what might happen in the future. When you are taking action, you are in the present. Leaving no room for fear.

The worst fear comes before you walk into a room. Once you start walking in, you then shift the fear from the act of walking to the obvious next step ... introducing yourself to someone you haven't met before. And, so it goes on. Once you have some momentum, you no longer fear the action you are taking. In listing the actions you can take when predicable fears arise, you are giving yourself an extremely helpful contingency plan - one that can stop you from overthinking or freezing in the moment. Instead you can recognise the situation you are in and instantly know the best action(s) to take. Having your backup plan in place can help you feel fully prepared and ready for anything, which in turn helps you to feel confident and in control.

Here are some of my coping mechanisms:

- When I feel anxious walking up to the Welcome Desk:
  - ➢ I walk more slowly and take three deep breaths as I go.
  - ➢ I go to the bathroom and secretly adopt a power-pose for two-minutes.
  - ➢ I offer to drive a friend to the event, so I do not have to walk in alone.

- When I'm worried I'll wear the wrong thing:
  - ➢ I look up photos from previous events online.
  - ➢ I ask someone who has been before.
  - ➢ I go for my favourite smart outfit.

- When I realise I don't know anyone in the room:
  - ➢ I stop, smile and take three deep breaths.
  - ➢ I start at the buffet table and ask a simple conversation starter question.
  - ➢ I scan the room for a small open circle, take a deep breath and walk in that direction.
  - ➢ I ask the person on the welcome desk for an introduction.

- When everyone looks more senior and experienced than me:
  - ➢ I remind myself of all the great conversations I have had in the past.
  - ➢ I run through a couple of affirmations in my mind.
  - ➢ I breathe deep, stand tall, smile and go for it!

Rehearse these strategies in your mind ahead of time. This will help turn these into them reflex actions, making it easier for you to follow through with your plan at the moment you feel your anxiety levels rising. Knowing you can handle these moments and obstacles will boost your confidence resulting in a much more enjoyable networking experience.

Rules: Giving yourself permission to proceed

When I started working on my networking skills in earnest, I struggled. I stressed out over what to wear, what to say, how to mingle, how to leave a conversation … everything! I decided to ask a colleague who LOVED networking if I could attend some events with her. I thought learning from her approach would be the solution I needed. I felt so relieved when, with a broad smile, she agreed to help me.

It was exciting and inspiring to accompany her as she danced from one group to the next. Sometimes engaging in more than one group at a time, leaning back to draw someone from different circle into her new conversation. It all came so naturally to her and she clearly revelled in every minute. The trouble was, as our personality types were polar opposites, I couldn't emulate her approach at all. It didn't feel possible, and I would not have come across as authentic had I tried. As grateful as I was for her support and encouragement, I had to find my own way.

That realisation came just days before I attended a leadership workshop, during which we were encouraged to try 'self-coaching'. We had to choose our own subject, something we have difficulty with. I chose networking. Then, taking a big step back from the issue, we had to brainstorm the steps we could take to overcome that problem. Once we were happy that we'd exhausted all our ideas, we had to go back through the list and determine which ideas were good. And then decide how we could start implementing them. It was a wonderful exercise and one I still use to this day to help me address my challenges objectively. Here's the list of viable actions that I created during that workshop:

The top five activities I can focus on to improve my networking:

- Find a good book which can teach me core networking skills.

- Network more and take note of what other people do that I like, and determine what I learn from them.
- Find one or two events I really enjoy and commit to going to these regularly.
- Once a week, invite a different colleague for lunch.
- Build my courage and confidence by attending something like a local drama group.

These actions served me well, with one exception. The last one. I really didn't like the idea of acting. But, when I spoke about it with one of the colleagues I had bravely invited for lunch, she gave me a better idea. Toastmasters.

Toastmasters is an international public speaking club that she had been meaning to attend for a while, so it was an opportunity for us to go together. It was perfect. I'll leave the full details of my Toastmasters experience for another day, but suffice to say I still attend to this very day. It's a wonderfully supportive network that helps you to grow at your own pace. I highly recommend that you find your local club and try it for yourself – but go at least three times before deciding whether or not it is the club for you. You can find a club at: www.toastmasters.org.

Thanks to my experiences there, I didn't just improve my networking confidence, I received some significant promotions in my corporate career. I developed the courage to accept international speaking opportunities. I was invited to become a TEDx speaker coach. And, I started my own podcast. These were all nerve-wracking, but wonderful experiences that I'm very grateful I was able to enjoy and I look forward to more of them.

There was one other concept I introduced, which aided my networking efforts. Rules. Knowing that I felt a certain amount of pressure when attending networking events, I wanted to find a way to give myself permission to learn and grow. Beating myself up at each fluffed introduction was holding me back, so I had to find a way to stop hindering myself in this way. So, I gave myself three rules. These served me really well. I would encourage you to create your own rules to support your growth too. Here are mine. You are welcome to use these if you feel they would also serve you, or create your own.

Rule 1 – Aim to Make Mistakes

I have come to learn that mistakes are good. We learn far more and grow more quickly from our mistakes than we ever will from getting things right all the time (which I am pleased to tell you that no one does). Our slip-ups and failures, from pushing boundaries and taking chances, give us valuable information and feedback that enables us to make adjustments as we move towards success.

When I did something that made me feel silly or awkward, which was a lot, I decided this was simply part of the process. Instead of worrying about it or vowing never to network again, I would simply reflect on what happened, and say to myself, 'Fascinating!' I would then determine what I could do differently next time, take a deep breath and move on, taking the lesson with me, but not the embarrassment. It worked like a charm.

Previously, each time I felt that I messed up, my inner dialogue would make me feel bad and hold me back more. I would even replay the incident over and over in my mind, causing me to dread my next networking encounter. There was really no constructive purpose in that. With hindsight, I don't think anyone else really noticed or cared about my errors anyway. None of them were as bad as I made them out to be in my mind. And we must remember, everyone is learning and everyone makes mistakes…even the 'professional' networkers.

I have since learned that this approach is being 'kindful' from a good friend of mine, Lynda Heffernan, an executive NLP coach and behavioural psychologist. We've had many fascinating conversations about what causes people to shrink back in fear or move forward with courage. These conversations always come back to this idea of being 'kindful' to yourself. This means, that whatever happens, you don't beat yourself up about it. Instead, you choose to look for the lesson and forgive yourself. Then leave your error behind you as you use your new understanding to grow stronger and more confident. As you adventure beyond your comfort zone, this idea of being *kindful* will be an important one to take with you.

Be aware of any times you catch yourself telling yourself anything less than encouraging, and look for a way to turn that around.

Rule 2 – Seek Experiences That Scare You

The second rule is more of a task. It was inspired by a quote from Eleanor Roosevelt: "Do one thing every day that scares you". I later learned that she was a classic introvert. She also hated networking but, in her later years, came to both enjoy and excel at it. I love the idea that this quote may well have been taken from her own set of rules created to help her build her confidence levels.

To start putting this rule into play, I made a list of all the things that scared me. I'm not talking about things like spiders, but regular activities that would push me outside of my comfort zone. I also included on the list, things to try for the first time. My aim wasn't to end up with completely tattered nerves, but more get comfortable with feeling a little bit nervous or awkward. I started with easy activities like making bread for the first time or trying out a new exercise class. Then I moved on to things I wanted to do, but didn't do, like inviting new people for lunch, calling someone instead of emailing them, or speaking up in a manager meeting. And then I did some of the scarier things, once I felt ready and a bit more courageous like giving a talk in French, hosting a live event or eating out alone.

Your list may be more or less courageous than mine. That's not what's important. What *is* important is to continually tip-toe, step or stride out of your comfort zone and, in doing so, expand it. The goal here isn't to change you, or turn you into someone that you're not, but to become your best-self so you can start achieving more of your goals and ambitions.

As I moved through my list, there were some activities that felt too big to tackle all at once. In those cases, I looked for ways to break them down into smaller parts. As the saying goes: 'What's the best way to eat an elephant? One bite at a time'.

For illustration, let me tell you about the time I gave a talk in French. In fact, I think this example brings together everything that we've discussed in this section of the book so far. I would love to tell you that I had the courage to give a lengthy talk in a foreign language to a room of hundreds of strangers. I didn't. But, as mentioned, that's not what matters. It's the act of following through on your intention, despite your fears that matters. This is where the growth is.

I spoke to a group of around 40 women at an event for the network that I had created. While I didn't know everybody in attendance, I knew enough of them to feel that they wouldn't judge me too harshly if I froze, forgot my words or had awful pronunciation. At the start of my talk, I asked them to bear with me as it was my first time speaking in French out loud to more than a couple of friends. Many in the room knew that just two years before, I hardly spoke a word of the language. I chose to learn Welsh at school instead of French. I remember thinking to myself 'when am I ever going to have to speak French?' I have been kicking myself over that decision for the last 16 years of living in French-speaking Switzerland! Anyway, back to my story.

When I gave my talk in French, I had a clear vision and goal. I wanted to make sure that those in the room who were native French speakers felt welcome. And I wanted to inspire the women to also step outside their comfort zone as they advanced along in their careers. This goal gave me the courage I needed to 'go for it'.

In my talk, I told them about my experiences as a woman in business. I shared the encouragement and wisdom I had been given that helped me to move forward. I also explained how I hoped my story would spark them to take charge of their own advancement. I spoke for a little over five minutes, but the women generously gave me a standing ovation … the ultimate confidence booster.

This leads me to another powerful lesson I have learned: when you share your story, experiences and vulnerability, it draws people to you. They will support and encourage you, and spur you on to your next step. It's a lesson that I have applied and seen work well in speaking, but also in networking, and it's the very lesson that inspired me to write this book for you.

Rule 3 - Celebrate Every Success

Confidence comes from having faith in your abilities. Therefore, an important part of confidence building comes from recognising your progress and achievements. With that in mind, my final rule was, and still is, to celebrate *every* success, no matter how small.

Before I implemented any of the strategies from my list, I considered how I would celebrate afterwards. This introduced the element of reward and, at times, that also helped me to be a little bit more courageous.

Sometimes, my steps offered their own rewards, like the wonderful friends I made along the way. Each of which I acknowledged with gratitude. Other times I would reward myself with small gifts. For example, if I successfully attended a certain event, I would have a glass of champagne when out with my husband instead of my usual glass of wine, or I would have a cocktail as an aperitif.

One thing I didn't do at the outset of my journey to courageous networking, was keep a success journal. A dedicated book, document or online tool where you keep a record of all the little things you're proud of or consider a success. This book will soon become a powerful tool for you, and it's why I've encouraged you to start a *Networking Success Journal*. Once you get in the habit of noting down your wins, your journal it will quickly become a great resource, particularly in those moments when your confidence waivers.

Rule 4 – Practice Gratitude

This wasn't one of my original rules. It is something that I added later that has helped me enormously. For that reason, I can highly recommend including it in your rules too. After each event, and at the end of every day, I take note of what I'm grateful for. These can be good things that happened, or things I was worried about that didn't happen – *have you ever noticed how most things we worry about never actually happen?* Sometimes I acknowledge the people who have supported me, or I give thanks for past, current or future opportunities.

You can be grateful for anything. It could be something as small as a smile someone gave you that lifted your spirits, or as big a landing a new client or contract. Size doesn't matter.

I mentioned earlier that where your attention goes, energy flows. In noticing the highlights of your life and experiences, you'll become a more positive and resilient person. You'll start to realise that your days have more highs than lows, giving you a more accurate perspective of what is possible for you. Plus, you will start to notice your courage grow as the grip your fears have over your ability to take action loosens. You see, you cannot hold thoughts of fear and gratitude at the same time! To get started, at the end of each day, note down three things you're grateful for. That's it. It only takes a minute of your time, but it can rapidly change your life for the better. You can use your *Networking Success Journal* for this. Turn it over so that the back becomes the front of the book, then start noting down what you are grateful for. Try it now! What three things are you grateful for today?

YES! You've Got This!

Every time you push outside of your comfort zone, you grow your beliefs regarding what's possible for you. In the coming weeks and months, if you follow this book and take action, much of what feels awkward and uncomfortable for you today, will start to feel (mostly) effortless and natural. I promise!

Too many people become stuck in a comfort zone that allows them to be average. But now you have the tools to ensure you don't fall into this trap!

You have a clear vision of a better future that you feel inspired and motivated to make happen. You have goals and know how you will achieve them, and who you will become in the process. You have a contingency plan to help you stay afloat when unexpected challenges threaten to halt your progress. You have rules to guide you and you have started a positive and powerful habit to help keep fear in its place. The only thing left to do is enjoy the journey!

Side-note: If you don't yet have all these things written down in your Networking Success Journal, then take some focused time to complete this before moving on. You will need this foundation if you are to truly succeed.

Assuming you have all these in place. It's time to pause, acknowledge your hard work and commitment, and celebrate. Once you have completed this final step, you are free to pass on to the second section of this book. I'm looking forward to sharing with you the hidden steps I have discovered to networking confidence and success! You've got this!

Part 2

MOVING INTO ACTION

"Once I discovered the three core elements of successful networking, I saw my confidence increase and my outcomes improve. This in turn built more confidence, and even better results. It's a virtuous circle and I'm excited for you to experience this for yourself."

Melitta Campbell

When I first started networking, I didn't put much thought into it. Like most people, I'd check I had enough business cards and then turn up. Walking into the room I always felt nervous and out of place. When asked, "What do you do?" I stumbled over my words, as though it was a completely unexpected question.

When it was my turn to speak, I'd ask some really feeble questions, leading to a short and uninspiring conversation before an awkward silence and an "I'm just off to the bathroom" exit. It was not fun, it was not fulfilling, and it was not effective.

Once I decided to change that and take my networking more seriously, things quickly started to change for the better. As mentioned in the first section of this book, simply *deciding* to do something is often enough to set you on a better path.

I split my efforts into three parts. Things I needed to prepare *before* an event. What to do *during* the event itself and follow-up activities to complete *after* the event.

I soon came to realise that it's what I did before and after the event that had the most impact – the two parts that I had completely ignored! Well, that's not strictly true. I hadn't ignored them; I was ignorant of them. It had never occurred to me that there was more to networking than just turning up with my business cards. I've since learned that I'm not alone in this respect. Whenever I speak or train people in how to network effectively, I always ask them what they do before and after an event. This question is usually met with silence and blank stares. However, more recently, some participants have raised their hands to tell me that they add all their new contacts to LinkedIn. On some occasions, someone will proudly explain how they accompany their LinkedIn invitation to connect with a personal message. It's a start, but there is so much more that can be done. And I can promise you that a little more effort leads to a lot more results.

What does an effective 'before' and 'after' event strategy look like? That's what I'll cover in this section of the book as I share what I have found most helpful. Once I started to work on my pre- and post-event actions, I saw my confidence increase and my outcomes improve which in turn built more confidence, and even better results. It's a virtuous circle and I'm excited for you to experience this for yourself.

Chapter 1

FIRST THINGS FIRST:
PRE-NETWORKING ACTIONS

"Pre-networking is key.
It sets up you for networking success."

Melitta Campbell

Creating your Milestones

Pre-networking is all about setting yourself up for success, which you explored in the first section of the book when you created your vision. But it's wise to break this down into a series of smaller milestones. This way, you can give yourself manageable goals to work towards.

Achieving these smaller goals will help you recognise that your efforts are paying off and will give you the motivation to keep going towards your next milestone, and so on. It will also give you cause for lots of celebration along your route to your ultimate goal – which is always my favourite part.

When I started to network in earnest, my first milestone was simply to feel comfortable walking into the venue, and engaging in one or two conversations. I didn't want to put myself under pressure to 'work the room'. All I needed was to get to know one or two nice people. It was a great feeling leaving an event knowing that I fulfilled my goal. Also, with the pressure to perform removed, I started to actually enjoy meeting new people.

Consider what your first few milestones could be, small actions or outcomes that feel manageable for you right now. Then note these in your *Networking Success Journal*. It can also be helpful to put dates or deadlines next to these so they become an 'action plan'.

Have an Event Objective

Networking can be described as 'conversation with purpose'. It's rare that we turn up to an event for no reason at all. When you are clear what that reason is ahead of time, you will be far more likely to come away having achieved something meaningful. Giving you more cause to celebrate.

The purpose is typically to grow your network, but it's worth spending a bit of time to think through what type of people you want in your network. For example, are you looking for someone who could be your mentor? Your supplier? Your business partner? Or, perhaps for someone who already knows a certain market? Or, someone who can help you with a current challenge you are experiencing? Or, maybe you'd just like some more local friends and contacts.

When thinking about who you want in your network, think widely. It's easy to surround yourself with a whole bunch of people who are just like you, but the best networks, like the best workplaces, are those that are diverse; filled with people that have a wide range of skills, backgrounds, experiences and influence that can supplement your own. It's even good to have people who think in very different ways to you, and can challenge your ideas to support you in creating robust well-thought-out solutions. Consider the gaps in your own perceptions, experience or understanding and seek out people who could step into those.

Today, whenever I have a challenge that's beyond my existing skills and knowledge, I always have someone in my network I can turn to for advice or guidance. They might not have the answers I need, but they can usually point me in the direction of the person that does. It saves me a lot of time and effort! It beats wading through the ton of content Google presents you with, particularly when it's not always clear what information is the most trustworthy or relevant.

Whenever I reach out to my contacts, I always come away with some amazing new insights and knowledge. At first, I was nervous about bothering other people by asking them for advice or guidance, but I've since come to understand that most people love to help others, and feel good about sharing their knowledge, experience and expertise. Just be sure that you share your insights generously too and always show your appreciation with a heart-felt 'thank you'. It's perhaps worth highlighting at this point, that one of the rules of good networking is to share value first. If you have adopted this approach, then when you reach out to your contacts for help, they will be happy to support you as you will have already have put some goodwill in the bank.

Practice Your Introduction

The question: "What do you do?" is inevitable when networking. Even so, it's a question that used to terrify me … I think it tapped into my fear that I wasn't good enough. It can feel daunting just walking into a networking event, but knowing you can introduce yourself clearly will give you an added dose of confidence and strip away at least one fear.

The key is to plan and rehearse ahead of time, so you don't get thrown off track when the question is asked.

I remember in my early days of networking, it never occurred to me to do this. As a result, I always felt flustered and mumbled something really dull in response, or waffled on for too long and felt stupid. Once I gave my introduction the appropriate preparation however, I not only started to build my confidence, but started to make more connections with the right people. Not just through the people I met directly, but from their referrals too.

Aim to keep your introduction simple and benefit focused. This means, instead of telling people what you do, tell them who you work with and what your clients or colleagues experience *after* working with you or using your products. It's much more interesting and memorable that way and, more often than not, it will prompt the question: "Ooh, how do you do that?" or occasionally "I really need that!" Responses like this give you permission to talk more about what you do, which is the outcome you really want. Talking about the benefits, instead of your job title, also ensures you to side-step any pre-conceptions they might already have about what you do.

For example, if you are a life coach, instead of saying "I'm a Life-Coach", you could say: "I coach busy female executives so they get more done, while feeling less stressed" – can you see the difference? Did it make you curious to know more?

Let's look at some more examples. If you're a bookkeeper, you could say, "I help business owners save time and improve cash flow". If you work in operations, you could say, "I prevent my colleagues from wasting time jumping through needless hoops". As a business coach, I tell people, "I guide purpose-driven women in how to confidently build a profitable business that gives them a balanced lifestyle."

While these phrases may seem simple, they can take a lot of time to create, play around with and perfect. It's OK if yours isn't quite as succinct as these examples - just don't make it too long or cumbersome to say. Keep it focused on *who* you work with and what they can look forward to (and possibly the pitfalls they avoid) after working with you. Practice saying it out loud to see how easily it flows and adjust as necessary.

I want to take a moment to highlight some of the things you should *never* say in your introduction, yet I hear people using far too often. Avoid say things like "I *just*…", "I run a *little*…", or "I do a *bit* of…" that undermines your talents, experience, or ability to get positive results. Be proud of what you do and the results you help your clients enjoy. If you appear doubtful in your abilities, others will doubt them too.

Also, avoid talking at length about everything you've achieved in the past. This rarely makes for an engaging opening. I remember speaking with a man who told me all about how he used to run this business and that department and all I was thinking was: 'But what do you do now?!' By all means talk about your background later if it's relevant or will build your credibility, but always start with who you are today and how you help your ideal client.

Study the Guest List
When building your network, you want to aim for diversity of background, industry, experience, knowledge etc. As highlighted above, this variety of perspective and experience will pay considerable dividends later on in your career or business development. You never know exactly where life will take you, so the more diverse your network, the more it will support you rising to the challenges and changes ahead.

To achieve this, study the guest list ahead of the event. Some events will give you a list of others who are attending in advance, and events with online registration often have a visible register of those who plan to attend. You can then do your homework and determine who you'd most like to meet. While you won't want to snub anyone at the event who isn't on your list, planning who you want to meet in advance will make it more likely that you'll achieve that aim. It can also guide you in how best to prepare what to say. This brings me nicely on to the next activity: preparing your conversation starters and maintainers.

Preparing Conversation Starters and Maintainers

Conversation starters are questions that you can ask to get an exchange going. Whereas conversation maintainers are stories, anecdotes or open questions that can be dropped into your discourse at suitable points to keep the conversation flowing and avoid any awkward silences.

If you know who is attending and who you'd be interested in meeting, you can research which openers and maintainers will be the most relevant. Use a tool like LinkedIn to study the people on your 'Would like to meet' list. Find out who they are, what they are interested in, what they have achieved recently, what articles they have written or shared and so on. Then use these insights to devise some appropriate questions, stories or reflections. This will help you feel composed and confident too.

In a good networking conversation, you want to speak for around 20% of the time, no more. People value being heard and enjoy being around those who listen and make them feel good about themselves.

This is a skill that comes naturally to many introverts. It also removes the pressure to 'perform' or be the centre of attention. So, speaking less and giving the other person the opportunity to speak more is really a win-win situation. When I learned this, I was so happy! I felt more at ease, and my new connections loved the attention they received. Giving people your time and focus really is a very special gift. It shows respect and it drastically improves your networking efforts. It's also much easier to remember who is who when you've shared an interesting discussion rather than just a passing comment.

That said, starting a conversation and keeping it going isn't always easy. This is something I struggled with for a long time, and I came to dread awkward silences. Once I started to equip myself with questions and stories that I had prepared in advance, however, I started to find myself enjoying my conversations much more, and relying on my classic bathroom excuse far less!

CONVERSATION STARTERS

Take some time to generate a list of open questions you can use during your conversations. Open questions are those that require more than a yes or no response. Here are some of the conversation starters that I have on my list. Feel free to use these to get you started:

- What is great with you today?
- How far have you travelled to be here?
- What did you think of the last speaker?
- What line of work are you in?

These can be followed by questions like:

- How did you come to be in your line of work?
- What do you like best about what you do?
- What other events do you enjoy attending?
- Have you read any interesting books lately? (be prepared to share a book you enjoy too?)
- Have you tried the buffet yet? Any recommendations?
- What types of projects are you working on?
- What exciting goals do you have for this year?

CONVERSATION MAINTAINERS

Stories and anecdotes are great for stimulating conversation. Look at some topical stories that you've enjoyed in the media that could be relevant to share at your next event – opt for those that are positive, short and easy to explain. As an introvert, I prefer to reflect on a question, concept or situation before giving my response. But, this doesn't work well in situations where you need to be spontaneous.

Sharing stories that I have pre-curated and practiced means I rarely feel anxious or 'put on the spot', and I can share my thoughts and questions with more confidence. As you collect your stories, keep note of any evergreen anecdotes or amusing stories with a moral that you can learn and use at any time or event.

One story I have been sharing for years and always gets people smiling is the one about the space race and the pen. It's perfect to use any time the conversation comes around to situations that have become over complicated, which is quite often! I've since learned that this story is a myth, but it still makes a good point in an interesting way and people relate to the moral nonetheless.

It goes something like this (feel free to use this yourself):

During the height of the space race in the 1960s, NASA scientists realised that their astronauts would need to complete paperwork daily, yet regular pens could not function in zero gravity. They spent years and millions of taxpayer dollars developing a ballpoint pen that could put ink to paper without needing gravitational force to pull on the fluid. Of course, the US astronauts weren't the only people with this challenge, the

Russians were also grappling with the same challenge. Their cosmonauts decided to use a pencil.

Have fun gathering a handful of stories like this, so you can mix your stories up. Then you're all set.

Preparing your Brand Stories

Another form of story that you can share that allows people to get to know more about you and the value you offer, are your own brand stories.

If your introduction is working as it should and your new friend has asked you for more information, you want to zoom in on just two or three of the key aspects of your work. You can then let them guide you with regards to which of those aspects they are most interested to know more about. Keep your responses relatively short and focused so there are plenty of opportunities for all those involved to share their views and ideas. There's nothing worse than someone hijacking the conversation and talking about themselves at length without a pause!

Think about some stories related to your work. These could be stand-out case studies, amusing anecdotes, lessons learned from times when things haven't gone according to plan, anything you feel is relevant and helps other people learn a bit more about your business, your value and what makes you stand out. You can even use hypothetical situations with great effect. Just be sure to make it clear that these aren't real by starting them with "Just imagine if…" or "Suppose…"

Keep a note of your stories and practice saying them out loud. This will ensure you always have plenty to share and talk about as and when relevant opportunities present themselves. However, don't ever feel you need to share all your stories at once. Remember that when you meet someone at a networking event, it's just the first stage of what may become a very long and happy relationship. So you can take your time.

I mentioned above that you shouldn't open with your past roles or achievements. However, they can make great stories that you can drop into your conversations as they develop. Sharing an experience and the lesson it taught you, for example, can be a powerful way to earn credibility and share something valuable.

Prepare Your Tools

THE BASICS: Remember to have your business cards at the ready, a fully charged phone and a pen and some paper just in case. A word of caution about cards – don't try and give out *all* your cards, instead offer them only to people whom you've enjoyed meeting and would genuinely like to speak to again. Make sure that it's one of the last things you do, and not the first. This makes it a genuine gesture rather than being taken as a desperate plea for more business.

If you were thinking of taking along a few brochures to the event too, don't. As mentioned, this is the very first stage of your relationship - you wouldn't propose marriage on a first date. If you meet someone who shows genuine interest in your business or what you do, it's far better to get out your calendar and arrange to meet them for a coffee to discuss things in more detail when you meet up.

YOUR WARDROBE: What you wear will not only influence what others think of you, but how you think about yourself too. Consider the impression you want to give to other people who may be meeting you for the first time, and what makes you feel comfortable and confident. There is no right or wrong here, but I would recommend checking that all your clothes are clean, and ensuring that you feel fully at ease in your chosen outfit. You don't want to be distracted by forgotten stains, shoes that pinch or a shirt that gapes in the wrong places.

YOUR ONLINE PRESENCE: Preparing your tools also means ensuring that your online presence is up to date and relevant to the people you are likely to (or want to) meet. This is the final stage of making a good impression as many of the people you meet will go and seek you out online before or after the event.

Check that your profile picture is current so it reflects how you look today so your new friends recognise you easily. Ensure that your straplines and headings are attractive to the people you want to meet. Consider sharing some relevant content on the day of the event that would catch their eye when they visit your profile...all the better if this is content that you have created or that invites them to join your email list. Go through all your profiles with a critical external eye and tidy up or update anything that doesn't speak to those who may be interested in learning more about you.

On your website, where possible, check that your lead-magnet or free offer is tailored to the interests of those at the event to increase your chances of turning eager visitors into loyal followers, supporters and possibly clients.

Prepare Your Mindset
We all have a little voice in our heads, like the angel and devil that appear on the shoulders of cartoon characters with a tough decision to make. Sometimes it shares helpful and encouraging advice. But all too often it fills our minds with self-sabotaging doubts, which can become self-fulfilling if we don't keep them in check.

Before you attend your event, remind yourself of your objective and why that's important for the achievement of your wider vision and goals. This will ensure you stay positive and stay motivated.

Then challenge yourself with this question. "Can I enjoy this networking event and come away successful?" Use it as an opportunity to remind yourself of all the reasons why yes, you can.

For example, your response might be: "Yes! I know who I'd like to meet and I have some information to share with them that I believe they will find stimulating. I know what questions I can ask to start fascinating conversations. I'm excited to wear my favourite outfit and make some new friends. I have a few new stories that I've found and practiced that I'm looking forward to sharing. Bring it on!"

Should you need a quick confidence boost before the event, Amy Cudy, author of Presence, suggests power posing. According to her research, if you can maintain a power pose for around two minutes, you give your body and mind a shot of testosterone that can give you a bit more courage. It's often, that's all it takes to get you in the room and starting your first conversation. Try going into a toilet cubicle and adopting a Wonder Woman stance with your legs strong and wide, your hands on your hips and your head held high. Watch Amy's TED talk for more on this.

Schedule Follow-up Time
Before you attend an event, already block out some time afterwards to follow-up on those you've connected with. If you don't, you'll find many of the new relationships you've started will fizzle out before they've had the chance to get started. We'll look at how best to use this time in the post-event section.

Minimise Novelty

While extroverts find that new experiences and high levels of stimulation give them energy, the opposite is true for introverts. We need time to absorb new things and situations. If there is too much going on at once, we introverts can quickly feel overwhelmed and exhausted. It can be helpful to minimise the effects of novelty on our senses, by acclimatising to new places and situations in advance.

For example, you could visit a new venue ahead of the event. Networking lunches and evenings are often in bars and hotels. Going there for a coffee a few days before would ensure that you can get familiar with the venue and its surroundings. If you're not able to visit the venue in advance, you could reach out to people who have been to the venue or event before, and ask about their experience. Was it easy to find? Where did they park? What were the people at the event like? If you don't personally know others who have been before, use the guest list. Scan those who plan to attend, and reach out to them through LinkedIn, MeetUp, and Facebook etc. This has the added bonus of ensuring you'll know some people when you arrive too. Seek out any details, even small ones that you can use to limit the amount of new information on the day of the event.

Knowing that as an introvert, you can feel drained when exposed to too much new information, try not to schedule anything new on the day of the event too. This will help preserve your energy stores.

I've experienced the impact of this reduction of novelty myself. I live in a small, but beautiful, Swiss town that borders Lake Geneva. Every year there are two big events here. The Montreux Jazz festival and the Montreux Christmas Market.

Today, I love both and find myself enjoying their buzz. But, I didn't at first. The first time I visited the jazz festival for example, I just went to one part where there was an open-air stage circled by a handful of bars and food stands. I enjoyed it, but had no desire to explore further. Also, I didn't stay all night like my friends either. Three hours was plenty, then I wanted to go home. As the years went on and I became accustomed to the crowds, sounds and activity, I'd explore more of the festival. Now I love experiencing all that the jazz festival has to offer. I'll move from one venue to the next in an evening. I'll enjoy discovering all the stands along the lake-front in one go. Sometimes I'll stay there from early afternoon until early the next morning. The last time I went, I even went on my own!

Plan Some Quiet Time

Finally, plan your day to ensure that you have some quiet time before the event. Introverts can find their system gets overwhelmed in loud and busy environments causing you to lose energy. Giving yourself some calm before the event will help you to feel your best when you arrive, and maintain your energy for longer. If you need to, it's perfectly acceptable to take a break during the event too. A short walk outside or taking some time out to read in a quiet corner can be just the ticket to recharge your batteries.

Following these preliminary steps will have a profound impact on your networking success. You'll be able to attract more of the right people into your network and being prepared will do wonders for your courage and confidence.

You now have everything you need to enjoy your next networking experience. So, let's take a closer look at what you can do during the event itself.

Chapter 2

MAKING FRIENDS: WHAT TO DO DURING THE EVENT

"As you attend events and put these into ideas into practice, you'll start to learn what feels natural and works best for you."

Melitta Campbell

Now you are fully prepared, looking good and have the recommended dose of courage on your side, the time has come to go to your next event.

Congratulations! This was the part that I always found the hardest, but once I used the VICTORY Formula and took the time to prepare my introduction, conversations and tools, that started to change.

That said, I still get butterflies from time to time, but no longer enough to bring me out in a cold sweat or derail my good intentions. In this next section, I want to share with you some of the tools and realisations that have helped me to navigate and succeed in these potentially awkward situations. As children, we were warned of the perils of speaking to strangers. For many of us, that fear has become deep rooted and can hold us back as adults. It's time to override that conditioning.

As you attend events and put these into ideas into practice, you'll start to learn what feels natural and works best for you. Keep track of your experiences in your *Networking Success Journal*. This will allow you to add to your tools and skills over time, and continue building your confidence and sense of ease. Remember to keep a note of and celebrate all your successes as you go.

Ta da. You've arrived!

Arriving at the venue can be the most daunting part. At least it was for me. Approaching the event, I'd find myself running through all the things that could go wrong. All the conversations I'd mess up. All the awkward silences I'd experience. All the blank stares I'd receive. All the people I'd insult by getting their name wrong, or by leaving a conversation … my list of impending disasters was endless!

In hindsight, it's obvious that this was the worst thing I could have done. Instead of taking this ill- advised approach, before *you* arrive at *your* event remind yourself of your vision, goals and all the reasons why 'yes, you can' enjoy a great event. If you have headphones or a stereo, you might like to create a 'feel good' playlist to listen to as you prepare for, or travel to, your networking adventure to help put you in the right frame of mind and keep 'the wobbles' at bay.

When you start your event with intention, a smile and an outstretched hand, everything else falls nicely into place. It's important to know and trust this. It will set you up for joy and success. So, take a deep breath and let's dive in.

Body language basics
We are instinctive creatures, and we often make immediate impressions of the people we meet. It is reputed that we do this within seven seconds!

Understanding some body-language basics can help you start to create meaningful connections, feel confident, and help others feel heard and valued while networking. The good news is that, whilst it may feel a little out of character at first, these are all simple strategies, and they all work. Put these techniques into practice consistently, and you'll soon find they become a natural part of how you 'show up'. Keep note in your *Networking Success Journal* of your personal observations as you try out these tools. Remember, you don't need to overwhelm yourself by trying everything at once. If it feels easier, pick out one or two things to try at a time.

When you feel shy or out of place, your body language can give you away. This is a problem on two counts. Firstly, when you make yourself small by crossing your arms and legs, you feel even less confident (and it's much harder not to stumble, especially if you are wearing high heels – trust me on that one!).

Secondly, when you display nervous body language, the knock-on effect is that others feel unsure around you too. Or they assume that you are unfriendly and to be avoided.

However, there is an easy fix. Instead of making yourself small, do the opposite by keeping an **open stance** when you speak with people. Stand up straight, pull your shoulders back and down, stand with your legs slightly apart, face the other person and keep your arms loose and not folded. You'll naturally feel stronger and more centred. Your open position will boost your self-confidence and make you look more open and confident to others too.

While this is a simple thing to do in theory, in practice it can feel a little unnatural at first, but you will soon get used to it. Practice standing in an open position at home, or while speaking with friends to start getting used to how it feels. I found the hardest part of maintaining an open stance was knowing what to do with my arms if they weren't crossed. I found the solution was to hold a glass – I discovered that soft drinks work best.

When speaking with people, maintaining good **eye contact** sends a powerful and positive signal. It demonstrates that you are interested in what the other person is saying, and assures them that you like who they are. This technique helps your new friend to feel comfortable and relaxed around you. Keep your focus gentle and natural. Avoid penetrating stares. Resist the urge to scan the room or to look over their shoulder when someone else is speaking. Wandering eyes make the other person feel under-valued or that what they are saying is uninteresting. That is not the impression that you would like to make.

Remember that your time and focus are the most precious gifts you give to others while networking. It's also about 'the Golden Rule', treating others with the same respect you would like to receive yourself.

Your **smile** is your secret weapon. When you smile, people tend to gravitate towards you. If in doubt at any time, just smile and see if people will share an involuntarily smile in return. Those that do are open to a conversation. Your smile is the best 'ice-breaker'. That said, you want to come across genuine and authentic, so avoid smiling too quickly. Instead, wait to give your smile in response to meeting someone or to something they have said. It's a small difference, but it will make the other person feel more appreciated and that will have a big impact.

I once had a colleague who had a big beautiful smile, only she never turned it off. Because she was already smiling when she saw you, she failed to make you feel that little bit special and valued. So, hold onto your smile for a moment, and then release it to show people that you are happy to speak with them.

This next technique may be something you need to work up to, but don't underestimate the power of **touch**. A study by the Cornell College of Hospitality, which researched the factors that cause waitresses to earn more tips, found that waitresses who touch a customer's hand or shoulder, earned an average of 25% more in tips. It clearly creates meaning for people. Just take care not to overdo it. I'm not a naturally 'touchy-feely' person, especially with people I don't know very well, but it's a highly effective way to create a connection. Always start with a firm handshake, and leave by touching their elbow or shoulder. It confirms that you've enjoyed meeting them.

I found this hard to do at first, but when I did it, the other person always smiled, and I felt surprisingly good. If you feel comfortable to do so, give the person next to you few gentle arm pats at relevant points in your conversation, and a longer connection when it's time to say goodbye. If you are in a circle of people, it's not necessary to touch everybody, just the person closest to you. Do this, but have eye contact with the others, and that touch will feel extended to them too.

On the subject of **handshakes**, make sure you have a good one! Start with a good posture, look the other person in the eye, reach out your arm and give a good firm, but not bone-crushing, handshake combined with a smile. This will indicate that you are trustworthy, warm and confident.

Another simple way to connect with people is to **mirror** their language and gestures. People are attracted to, and feel comforted by, those who are like themselves. While you don't want to be insincere, a copy-cat or to try and be someone you're not, aligning your behaviours to those of the people around you can help you to fit in and connect quickly. 'Mirroring' is instinctive, so you may find that you already do this naturally. And definitely no **yawning**! That's a sure-fire way to offend the other person. If you feel a yawn coming on, do what The Queen does and fold your tongue, this will help stop the yawn. Just reading this has probably brought on a yawn, I know I am while typing this, so give this tip a try now. Cool, right?!

Remembering Names

I've talked a lot about how important it is to create connection and to ensure that the people you meet feel valued. One of the key ways of achieving both is to remember names. When you call someone by their name, it gives them a moment of recognition…something we all crave. This is easier said than done for most of us, but here are some techniques that I have found work well.

Take a moment to look at how their name is written on their name badge. Often seeing a word helps you to remember it. If they have an interesting name, or spelling, comment on that. It will help lock their name into your memory, and it's an easy conversation starter. "I haven't seen Alys written with a 'Y' before, it's so pretty that way. Is there a story behind that?"

Try and say their name at least three times. Once you get into the habit, weaving someone's name into your comments becomes quite easy: "Hi Ellen, it's so nice to meet you. So, Ellen, tell me more about what you do." "…that's so interesting Ellen, you must love what you do." "Ellen, I just love what you shared there…" "Ellen, I've loved our conversation today. I look forward to speaking again soon."

Make a connection between their name, and one of their attributes. Maybe Wendy wore a skirt you could imagine blowing about when it's windy. Maybe Ellen had light blonde hair like the talk show host. Perhaps you can imagine Tiffany looking through a jewellery shop window. Get creative and have fun with this one.

Remember people are just people

People are just people; even at a networking event. While you may feel you are the only one who is nervous, the truth is, many people feel intimidated by these events and will be feeling exactly the same way as you do. Consider each "Hello" as a service that helps others feel at ease. As this is the very first step in what could be a long and happy friendship, it's helpful to imagine you are talking to a potential friend, not someone with a dollar sign on their head. I'm sure you won't have to think back too far, to recall a time when you have been networking and someone treated you in that way, and how artificial an exchange it was. This is the time to reach for one of your prepared conversation openers to kick-start a great networking experience.

Scan for 'open circles'

'Open circles' are small groups of people that have been left slightly open to allow others to join in easily. When you arrive at your networking event, take a moment to scan the room for an open circle. That is always the easiest place to start. When you join, it's polite to smile and say 'Hello', but wait for a pause in the conversation before properly introducing yourself.

Start the conversation

I used to find it hard to start a conversation with new people. I'd say "Hello" and then I'd tense up as I searched my mind for something clever to say next, only to find that all my thoughts had been stolen clean away by 'Mr Fear' and 'Mrs Doubt'! I was left feeling awkward and self-conscious. These acute feelings prevented me from connecting with people and I struggled to process or respond to their side of the conversation. Here is how I overcame these harrowing situations:

Breathe deeply.

As mentioned previously, three deep breaths can help you to feel instantly calmer and more centred. Breathing is one of the key techniques I've used to overcome most of my emotional barriers so, apologies if I seem to over-recommend this strategy. I suggest you research the multiplicity of advice there is on appropriate breathing for mastering a host of different challenges.

Smile and wave.
In the film Madagascar, Skipper, the leader of the penguins, advises his friends to "Smile and wave boys, smile and wave". This was to distract zoo workers and visitors from the fact that they were digging an escape tunnel. It's a technique I often use while networking to distract from my nerves. Of course, smiling and waving would be a bit odd in this context. Instead, it's more of a 'smile and shake'. But saying '*Just smile and wave boys*' in my mind gets me moving and stops me from overthinking. Then I can simply walk up to someone, smile, extend my hand and say "Hi, I'm Melitta", and that's it, conversation started.

Focus on the other person.
Think about what you can do to help the other person feel at ease. Give them a warm smile, and ask some easy to answer questions to help you find some common ground, like a mutual experience or point of view.

When I started to do this, I found it so much easier to network. Shining the light on someone else's experiences and achievements helped me to avoid the limelight, which put my introverted soul at ease. As I've already touched on, people crave recognition, even if they aren't aware of it, so giving them space to share their stories and opinions makes them feel great. People love to be around people who make them feel good about themselves.

Keeping it going

Once your conversation is underway:

Give your full attention.

Your time and attention are the most valuable things you can give to anyone. When getting to know someone, it's important actively listen. This requires you to focus on what they are actually saying, rather than on planning what you will say next. Demonstrate that you are giving your full attention by turning your body towards them and maintaining eye contact while they speak. Smile and nod to reassure them you are enjoying their contribution.

Allow others to join the conversation.

When networking in a group environment, leave room for others to join your discussion by keeping your circle open and welcoming newcomers with a smile. At a relevant break in the conversation, introduce yourself and tell them what you are discussing so that they can join in too. Doing this not only brings others into the conversation, but has the benefit of positioning you as a considerate professional who is worth getting to know.

Be animated and passionate.

People will often judge you on your energy so don't shy away from showing your enthusiasm for a subject. Energy is highly engaging, infectious and memorable. It will also build credibility and trust as you just can't fake genuine interest. As introverts tend to be on the quieter side, find and discuss topics, stories and concepts that spark your excitement or curiosity. This is where your prepared stories can really come into their own. If you find your energy dipping, go for a short walk alone to recharge.

Let people speak.

While showing enthusiasm is great, avoid getting so excited that you interrupt others in conversational flow. This is disrespectful and rarely wins you favour. A better approach is to focus on what it being said, and then when it's your turn, acknowledge what you liked or agreed with, then add your perspective or story if it adds value and furthers the conversation.

Encourage the flow.

Keep your conversations alive by asking simple open questions, such as "What did you think of the presentation?", "How does this compare to the other networking events you attend?" and follow-up responses like "How did that feel?", "That's so fascinating, what happened next?" Bring other topics into the conversation too to keep it alive. Perhaps some areas of common interest have become apparent that you can explore. If not, you can use some of your planned stories and questions.

Here's a little secret I've learned; giving someone three nods at the end of their sentence signals that you like what they have said and are happy for them to continue, helping to keep the conversation flowing with ease. Try it out!

Create connection.

Highlight areas of commonality, as they arise. People find it easier to connect with those who hold similar views, backgrounds or experiences. It's always interesting to see how much you have in common, even with people who seem completely opposite to you. You can make a game of trying to find your personal connection with each person you speak with. Bring some more personal questions into the conversation as it continues to help find and build more connection.

However, questions around their private life, religious or political views are best avoided; unless linked to the subject of the event itself.

Avoid negative conversations.
Every now and again, you'll find yourself in a discussion that takes a negative turn. You want to avoid getting drawn into these mood-altering conversations. They rarely feel good and they are terrible for your brand. Even if it's someone else's pessimistic views, by commenting or even just being in 'the circle', others will start to associate you with the same view point. To remove yourself from a negative conversation, simply smile, say 'thank you' and then walk away and find a new conversation to join.

Your Communication and Words
For more than 25 years, I've studied and worked in marketing and communications. Along the way I've picked up a few little tricks that you can use in your networking to create a lasting impression. Here are my favourites:

Put them first. People are always most interested in learning about how your offering affects them. Once they know this, then they will be interested in how that event, product or initiative impacts their community (their family or team for example). Lastly, they will be interested in how it affects their wider community, such as their company, industry or country. With this in mind, always share your stories and comments that way around, starting with how it impacts or benefits them as an individual.

Keep your words simple.

We're often tempted to impress by using long or complicated words. But even in report writing this rarely works. Aim to use the same words and conversational tone as you would when speaking with a friend over coffee. Simple always works best in communication. A confused mind does not buy, or buy-into anything!

Interestingly, words of one syllable are extremely easy for the brain to process, so phrases made up of simple words are quick to memorise. This is probably why to this day you probably remember lots of nursery rhymes, lyrics like Kylie's 'I just can't get you out of my head,' or famous lines like 'I have a dream' or 'We will fight them on the beaches'. Use this fact to your advantage by constructing your important messages from simple words.

Making key points memorable.

There are three ways you can encourage people to remember important points. Make it rhyme, use words of one syllable and /or make it a short sound bite or story. You'll need to plan, prepare and practice these ahead of time to achieve this result, but it can be worth doing if your key point is related to your brand, product or company.

Another option is to use the power of three. You may have noticed that I did this three times in the paragraph above. Our brains are trained to process patterns, and three is the smallest pattern you can create. Experiments have shown that patterns of three are consistently the most pleasing and the easiest to remember. As above, you may want to prepare this in advance to help people absorb your key points by weaving patterns of three into your prepared stories or even your introduction.

Keep it positive.

Even when speaking about negative things, you want to use positive language such as 'avoid' instead of 'don't', 'remember' instead of 'don't forget', 'it's a pleasure' instead of 'no problem'. For one, it makes your words easier to process and act upon as our brains struggle to process negative concepts. But more importantly, people tend to fuse your message and words with your character, so it's important to ensure that your phasing reflects how you want to be known.

Moving on from a conversation

This is something that I struggled with for a long time. I was plagued by the question of how to move on to a new conversation without appearing rude. I tried just staying with someone and not moving on. But when a conversation came to a natural end, there was that inevitable 'awkward silence'. I often resorted to the, 'I'm just going to the Ladies' trick, which felt like a complete cop-out unless I really did need to go to the bathroom. Sometimes I mixed things up by saying, 'I'm just going to the bar', but that was not without its challenges either. However, I soon realised, that this exit plan requires you to offer to get the other person a drink too, and to then continue the conversation on your return! So, maybe after another drink the bathroom excuse could be at least genuine.

It is natural for conversations to fizzle out. You are at the event to network after all. So, moving on from a discussion is accepted behaviour. It's helpful to remember this. However, since last impressions can count as much as first impressions, aim to leave on a positive note. Here's how…

Wait for a natural pause in the conversation before making your exit. Then thank the person, or group, for sharing their insights and mention something that you will enjoy taking away with you. For example, "I've really enjoyed this discussion. I'll be sharing that story about the space pen with my colleagues tomorrow! I look forward to speaking with you again soon." Or, perhaps refer back to something they shared: "Good luck with your podcast interview next week. Do share the episode with me once it's published, I'd love to listen to it and share it with my network".

You can also give a reason for your departure. Perhaps you want to go and get a seat in the auditorium before the main event starts. Or, maybe you have a babysitter to get back to or another meeting to attend. Giving a reason implies that you'd really love to keep speaking with them, which has a nice feel-good factor to it. Just be sure that your reason is genuine.

If you haven't already done it, your exit statement would nicely dovetail with asking for their contact details, exchanging business cards or adding them directly as a contact on LinkedIn.

Here's my favourite exit strategy. When it's time to move on, finish your conversation as above, and then say: "I'm going to mingle a bit more – before I do, what kind of contacts are you hoping to meet this evening? If I meet anyone that meets that profile, I'll be sure to introduce you!" If you feel comfortable, lightly touch their elbow when you say this, it will come across as all the more warm and sincere.

This parting note has many advantages: they will be happy to let you go and mingle as you'll be helping their networking efforts too; it will invite them to do the same for you; it will make you stand out as very few people say something along these lines; and it makes you look incredibly considerate and professional.

Finally, finish by leaving the door open: "Great! And I'll be in touch to arrange meeting up for that coffee."

Another alternative is to take them with you. This is particularly appreciated by those who are also nervous or feeling out of place.

"Shall we mingle some more? We can go together!"

Leaving the event

Before leaving the event, aim to say goodbye to the people you've met and thank them once more for their time and conversation. Where you can, use their name in your farewell. Where appropriate, reaffirm that you are looking forward to staying in touch or meeting up for coffee. Though only do this if you genuinely plan to follow up. Otherwise, a simple "goodbye, it has been nice meeting you" will suffice.

Finally, always make a special effort to say goodbye to and thank the organisers. Often the organisers are volunteers, and always put in a lot of time and effort into making sure the event is a success, so taking time to say thank you is always appreciated. This simple gesture also helps you to be remembered positively with two great benefits.

Firstly, it will make it easier to attend your next event, as the organiser will remember and welcome you. Secondly, having created a good impression, the organiser will often introduce you to the people worth knowing the next time you attend. It's worth planning an extra 15-minutes for your goodbyes so that you are not rushed as you leave.

How did that feel? You see, networking needn't be so hard or scary. The more you put these tips into practice, the easier it will become.

With your event being over, the next step is to follow up. This is the most important stage! As the saying goes: 'The fortune is in the follow-up'.

Chapter 3

FIRMING UP YOUR FRIENDSHIPS: POST-EVENT ACTIVITIES

"How you follow up with your connections determines just how successful your networking outcomes will be."

Melitta Campbell

You've prepared well and attended your networking event. Now it's time to start turning all your new connections into meaningful relationships. How you follow up with your connections determines just how successful your networking outcomes will be.

It's really important that you don't just go out and meet people, but that you make them an active part of your network by continuing the conversation after the event too. The fortune is in the follow up! The good news is, this part plays to our strengths as introverts. Most of us like to reflect before speaking or sharing insightful information, and in your follow up activities, this is a great asset. This is the moment when you can really shine.

I always make an effort to follow up with the contacts that I want to stay in touch with within a week of the event and at regular intervals. It's helped me to build a solid network over time. Though, I can count the number of people who have followed up with me on my right hand!

Few people make the effort to nurture their network, so it's an easy way to stand out from the crowd and make sure that at the next event, you will meet up with many familiar friends instead of a roomful of strangers.

Here are some thoughts on following up after the event:

Follow up thoughtfully
You want all your follow up to demonstrate two things. Firstly, that you value having your new contact in your network. And secondly, how you can be a valuable part of theirs.

With this in mind, as well as sharing articles and information you believe they will find interesting and helpful, you also want your subsequent points of contact to help them get to know more about you and what you stand for.

A short, but thoughtful email or a direct social media message, to one person will have far more impact than a mass email. Particularly when your objective is to build the foundations for a lasting relationship. Set time aside to send out a personalised message. You don't have to follow up with everyone you met, just those with whom you'd like to stay in touch with.

Thank the organiser

Organising events is hard work. As well as thanking the organiser when you leave the event, it's good practice to also send them a message the next day to let them know how much you appreciated their hard work. If you want to really stand out, you can thank them in a social media post too, including a link to the next event to help them with their promotional efforts. Then you'll always be remembered for the right reasons.

"Amazing Conference was great last night. I learned so much about xxx from the speakers and have made some wonderful new friends. A big shout-out to Joe Bloggs and Jenny Jones for putting on such a valuable event. I'm looking forward to the next one on June 10th, who else is going to join me? Here's the link to all the details: xxx."

Keep track of your contacts

As your network grows, keep on top of your contacts by developing a system for recording and categorising everyone you know. There are many ways to do this, from using an online CRM or project management tool like Trello, to a simple spreadsheet, dedicated notebook or rolodex. There is no right or wrong way, so go with the type of system that feels most manageable for you.

I had one boss who kept a profile sheet on everyone he met. After each meeting, he'd update the appropriate page and refer to his notes before his next meeting with that person. I remember feeling so valued when he started each meeting with a question that followed-up on our last conversation. It's perhaps no surprise that during his career he had a series of very senior positions for some of the world's leading companies.

Your record should include the name, contact details, family information, interests, achievements, and skills of each contact. It can also be useful to categorise each contact (close friend, colleague, occasional acquaintance etc.). Keep a note of the last time you met, what you discussed, and a thoughtful question to ask when you are next in touch. You can do the same thing if you are adding a contact to your phone. Instead of just adding their name, add a note.

For example, Jenny could be Jenny 'cupcakes', Bob might be Bob 'storyteller', then when they call you or you call them, you can use this information: "Hey Jenny, made any new cupcake flavours recently?" Being able to recall such information when you meet people will help them to feel valued and cement your relationship. It will also help with your own confidence too.

Regularly share information
A willingness to share is at the heart of successful networking. When you come across new information or something that makes you think or makes you smile, take a moment to consider if others in your network might also benefit from receiving it. The more you share with others, the more they

will share with you in return. But, it must be relevant to that person and you must write at least one sentence to explain why you are sending it to them – unsolicited, random or 'cut and paste' messages are considered spam and are rarely appreciated.

Always use their name
As I've mentioned before, the sweetest sound to any person anywhere in the world is the sound of their own name; it's also the best way to grab their attention - never miss a chance to use a person's name.

Follow through on your promises
If you promised to send your new contact a particular article, more details about your product, or arrange a time to meet for a coffee, then be sure to do that. So many people fail to make good on their pledges, so this is another chance to stand out as a person of integrity.

Following through, also refers to you. Did you promise yourself something nice if you succeeded with your networking? A new notebook, your favourite cocktail, a massage… Remember to make good on your promises to yourself as well. This will build your confidence as you reinforce that you are worthy of praise, investment and recognition.

So, that's follow up. Don't allow the short nature of this last section to fool you. As I said earlier in this book, it is the MOST important and impactful part of your entire networking process. Be sure to give it the time and focus required to do it well. Then enjoy all the new connections and opportunities that you've created. You'll be amazed how far they will take you in business and in life.

Chapter 4

CREATING YOUR SUCCESS CIRCLE

"No one succeeds in a vacuum.
Having a core group of supporters will be
essential to your ongoing success."

Melitta Campbell

I wanted to introduce a powerful concept that I encourage all my clients to embrace: creating a Success Circle.

Your Success Circle is the inner-sanctum of your network. It's a small group of one to five people who are there to champion you and your business every step of the way – and for whom you are willing to do the same. No one succeeds in a vacuum, so this core group of supporters will be essential to your ongoing success.

Your Success Circle can be made up of peers, mentors, coaches, supporters, or partners. There are no hard and fast rules here. Your core group should consist of people who believe in you and your business, understand and back your mission, inspire you to step up into your potential (while embracing your true self), and are there for you in the moments when you need them most.

Of the eighty, and counting, successful women I've interviewed for my Driven Female Entrepreneur podcast, most of them attribute part of their success to not just having a strong network, but also a handful of core connections who have supported their journey.

Few people have a fully-formed success circle from day one. Therefore, it's something that will develop as a result of your networking efforts. Keep an eye out for potential success-circle members, but allow the right friendships to develop naturally. There is no deadline for having your circle in place. But when you do, you'll enjoy the benefit. Members of your core group may change over time. This is perfectly normal.

As with all your relationships, add thoughtful value regularly, so your Success Circle know you value them. And enjoy the feeling of security and fulfilment that it brings.

Chapter 5

ONLINE NETWORKING

"Online networking is growing in importance.
Much of what you've already learned from
this book, works equally well, if not
better, when networking online."

Melitta Campbell

I live in an area where most of the local business networking events take place in French. While this is a language I can now speak reasonably well, keeping up with a full-speed conversation is still a challenge. I also have a travelling husband and young family, meaning that I can't attend as many in-person networking events as I might like.

As a result, for more than a decade, I've been making full use of online networking opportunities to build and grow my connections. From these experiences, I've learned that most of the advice I've already shared with you, works equally well, if not better, when networking online.

Seeing as online networking is growing in importance, especially since the arrival of the coronavirus, I'd like to take a moment to highlight some practices I've found work best. You'll recognise many of them

Preparation

If you are going to network with people online, first be sure that all your profile information is up to date and relevant. This ensures that when your new contact checks you out, which most will, they get the right impression and are eager to connect. Having an attractive profile, with clear links through to more information about your business and areas of expertise or interest, will also attract inbound enquires too. In other words, people who are interested in or looking for your skills and services will come to you. The clearer and more focused your content and profile, the more people will come your way.

Remember people are still people

While you may be communicating via your computer and keyboard, or smart device, you are still reaching out to *people*.

Forgetting this is the biggest mistake I see being made online. Just as with in-person events, you want to keep in mind the people you want to meet, what would be meaningful for them, and the impression you want to leave them with.

Add value first
This should be at the core of your online networking efforts. The good news is, it's incredibly quick and easy to do. Look for meaningful ways you can add value to the people you would like to get to know, have recently met, or who are established members of your network. It's worth setting aside time to do this regularly. Dedicating just 10 minutes a day to value-adding activities, for example, will soon add up to a powerful difference and will ensure you stand out for the right reasons. It can be helpful to keep a list of people you would like to focus on, so you can strategically build a strong network.

There are three key ways to add value. Firstly, you can share interesting articles via private social messages or email. When doing so, be sure to explain why you thought it would be of value. For example, with a new contact you could say, "I found your recent post on authentic sales extremely interesting. It made me think of this research from Clever Lab, have you seen it already?"

Secondly, you can share their content with your audience. This takes seconds to do, but will gain you a lot of goodwill. It takes time to create a meaningful video, podcast episode, blog article or even a long-form social media post. When you share it with your audience, it gives the author recognition and greater visibility. Two highly valuable commodities online.

If you share someone's content on social media, be sure to tag them in the post and send them a personal note to tell them why you found it valuable enough to share. This will give you a powerful first contact or follow up. To come across as authentic to your audience (i.e. your existing network) and your new contact, only share content that you genuinely find interesting and feel that your audience will also enjoy.

Finally, like and comment on their social media posts. Again, this shows that their work is appreciated and increases their reach online. Be sure that your comments are meaningful however. Aim to use at least five words and avoid phrases like: "This is great, thanks for sharing", instead go for something more relevant or better still, something that will prompt a discussion such as: "What a great article. I particularly resonated with point six, I am always getting spammy messages on LinkedIn. Why do you think so many people think this approach works?"

Keep your conversations short
People have less time (and patience) online. With this in mind, for the best results, avoid long messages. Take your time to get to know your new contacts. It's best to build rapport over a series of short bites of information and easy to answer questions, instead of overwhelming them with one long 'catch all' message. It's harder for people to follow your content online, as your words aren't accompanied by helpful visual or vocal clues. Therefore, keeping your messages short, clear and to the point will greatly aid comprehension too.

Just as during an in-person conversation, be sure to give the other person your full attention, read their message fully and give a response that indicates that you have understood and valued what they have shared with you. This will help keep the conversation flowing.

By taking your time to 'talk' to your new contacts in a natural way, that reflects a real conversation, you will be able to find common ground, understand their ambitions and interests, explore synergies, and identify ways you can support them. Bear in mind that the best partners for your business are those with shared values; people will only refer you once they know, like and trust you; and you can only sell to people with their permission. Therefore, taking your time to understand the situation, viewpoints, expertise and needs of your new contacts, will put you in a stronger position to grow your business via your network.

Share valuable content

The beauty of social media, is that you can attract people to you by sharing valuable content on topics that are relevant to your ideal clients. While much of your online networking will involve you proactively reaching out to others, remember that you also want to encourage people see you as a valuable person to get to know, and reach out to you too.

Open circle content

Remember how we talked about looking for open circles when you enter a networking environment? You can recreate this online by asking simple questions on your social media posts, and inviting people into a conversation around that topic. For example, "When was the last time you gave out a business card?" or "Fill in the blank, Networking means_____". This type of content is highly engaging and allows you to get to know your existing contacts better. It also invites new people into the conversation. Be sure to connect with any new people who join your 'circle' and start a discussion with them though the messaging function to build the relationship

Use groups

Find online groups and forums that discuss topics that are interesting to you and your ideal connections. These are going to be hot beds of relevant contacts. Remember to share value first, and reach out to people who seem particularly relevant, keeping the conversation short and relevant.

You can even create your own groups. This way you can stay highly focused on the themes that your ideal clients and connections would find valuable, and attract the network to you.

Rented ground

One thing to keep in mind with online contacts, is that you don't own the lists you create. For example, you may have five thousand connections on LinkedIn, but if your account is hacked or closed down for some reason, you will lose these overnight. Therefore, it's important to find ways to add your contacts to your email list or a good old-fashioned rolodex – with their permission of course. Using lead magnets or hosting events that people need to register for, for example, are two of the many ways you can do this.

Meeting for real

While online platforms make it easy to network with people at any time any place, the best connections and deepest relationships always come from in-person networking. So always look for opportunities to meet your connections in person, or in a one-to-one discussion through a tool such as Zoom or Skype. Remember, confidence is dynamic, so it's important not to rely on online networking too much, you'll risk losing the skills and confidence you've built to date. As the saying goes: 'Use it or lose it'.

Chapter 6

NETWORKING AND YOUR PERSONAL BRAND

*"Since you want to encourage people to
speak about you to others, your
personal brand is very helpful to
consider carefully and consciously build."*

Melitta Campbell

I believe that building your personal brand and networking can be a powerful combination. While I've touched on some elements of personal branding throughout this book, I wanted to collate them all together here too, so you can use them to your full advantage.

When I talk about your personal brand, I'm not talking about a specific colour palette or logo – though you could use these to stand out if you wanted. What I'm really looking at is what you are known for and what you mean to other people.

Given that definition, you already have a personal brand. If someone from your network were to recommend you to someone else – how would they describe you? What would they say about your areas of expertise? Your ability to get results? Your personal traits? That is your personal brand. And since you want to encourage people to speak about you positively, and in ways that bring about the results you want for your career or business, it's something that is very helpful to consider carefully and consciously build.

Here's the thing. If you don't manage the way you appear to others, they will form their own opinions of you, which may or may not be how you want to be remembered. Run through a few of the names in your network, how would you describe them to others? That's *their* personal brand. How did you form that opinion? Most probably from the way you have seen them behave, the conversations you've had, the type and usefulness of the content they've shared, and their follow-through on promises. Can you see how the way you network, can affect your personal brand?

Here's the challenging part about brands – personal or otherwise – you don't own them. Your brand is how other people perceive you in their mind. That's why building a brand takes time and consistency.

If each of your messages sound completely different from the last one, if you are in a different mood every time people meet you, or if you cover a wide array of topics, it's hard to stand out and be known or remembered for anything in particular making it hard for your contacts to refer you to others.

The good news is that building your personal brand needn't be difficult. It's not costly either. It's about you showing up as your best self, consistently - the entire theme of this book.

At its simplest, this means being clear about several things:

- The two or three topics or expertise you want to be known for
- The values and ideals you live by
- Why you do what you do
- Your goals and why these matter to you, and
- How you want to be remembered, so you can behave accordingly.

Once you are clear on these points and are congruent with them, you'll be remembered for your integrity and your network will confidently refer you to their contacts.

For example, for my personal brand, which is very closely aligned to my business brand, I've noted that I want to be remembered as a business coach with a specific passion for: making marketing simple for small businesses, helping people communicate their value clearly and with confidence, and as a champion for female-owned businesses.

This means, that I need to ensure that all my content and follow up messages come from at least one of these three perspectives. This is actually fairly easy, as these subjects lie close to my heart and reflect a life-time of experience. I also use a tone of voice that reflects the right personality. For me, this means expressing my thoughts and insights in the same way I would with a friend over coffee. Using clear, simple and engaging words and phrases. And including short stories and anecdotes where they aid clarity or impact.

Take a moment to think about what your personal brand is. Consider the questions listed above to help you. Write your answers down in your *Networking Success Journal*. Building your personal brand takes time. It's something you need to reinforce overtime by acting in accordance with your brand through all your interactions and appearances, everywhere.

If you've built your brand around your values and personality, then this should be straight-forward to achieve.

As I've mentioned throughout this book, it's important to be true to yourself. You'll always 'do you' best. In building your personal brand, avoid the temptation to feel you have to be more like anyone else. Embrace all aspects of your character, including the imperfections, these are often what make you most relatable.

Enjoy exploring all that it means to be you. Then step into that and 'do you' on purpose.

Chapter 7

CONCLUSION

*"The path you are about to travel has
many unexpected, yet wonderful, twists
and turns that will reveal themselves
at the most unexpected, yet perfect times."*

Melitta Campbell

While I may have grown up 'the shy girl', I've always enjoyed being around others. So, despite my fears and challenges, I was delighted when I finally started to feel more at ease and enjoy networking.

Over the years, it has opened a variety of doors for me, often in unexpected ways.

As you've probably gathered by now, this was far from an overnight process. Networking is a skill that I've needed to consistently work at to maintain a certain level of confidence. There have been moments when I've been complacent and haven't followed the processes outlined in this book. Those are often the times when things haven't gone as well as I'd have liked. When this happens, I remind myself that it's OK. I am only human and I'm not going to 'hit the ball out of the park' every time. These moments also remind me why having a process – even (or especially) a very simple one – is so important.

It prompts me to review my vision and goals, as created through my VICTORY Formula. I can then look ahead and map out the outcomes I want to create as a result of my networking efforts, and determine the connections and stories that will help me achieve this. While doing so, I'll also check if everything is still in alignment. As my personal and professional world has expanded, sometimes I've found that my vision, goals and stories needs to shift in response to this. You'll want to check this regularly too. After all, if you've been following the steps in this book, you haven't just developed your networking skills, you will have also attracted new knowledge, insights and possibility into your life through the connections you've made, catalysing growth. If you've been taking action while reading this book, even if some of that action is visualised rather than played out for real, you are not the same person right now, as you were when you first picked up this book. Have you noticed that? If not, take a read through your *Networking Success Journal* to see how far you've already come!

Looking back over my journey, I never imagined myself being where I am today. But, I haven't arrived here alone. I'd love to conclude this book by introducing you to a handful of the people who have inspired and supported my journey, and the places these connections have taken me. You'll soon see that the path you're about to travel has many unexpected, yet wonderful twists and turns that will reveal themselves at the most unexpected, yet perfect times.

My journey began in earnest when I moved to Switzerland. I had no connections here, so I had to start from scratch - probably the biggest catalyst of them all! I had no choice but to push myself to learn the skills and get out there. Much like the day I arrived at my university halls.

When I adopted 'Rule 2' and started inviting my colleagues for lunch, I met Tammy. She was a fellow Brit and an energetic lady with an infectious appetite for learning and adventure. When I mentioned that I'd been looking at ways to improve my presentation skills, she told me about Toastmasters. She'd been meaning to give it a try, and so we went to our first meeting together. That was the start of my career development and public speaking journey. It didn't end there. Tammy was also the person who introduced me to women's networks. Up until then, I hadn't really seen the value of them, but after attending an event together, I was hooked. We later worked together to set up a women's network within the bank, with the purpose of empowering and connecting women, and prompting positive change. The network provided me with many life-changing experiences and taught me a lot about what it takes for women to succeed, insights I still use in my work today.

Keen to expand my professional network, I reached out to Susan, head of communication for a large multinational company. I'll never forget how generous she was in sharing her time, significant wisdom and encouragement. While we met through our common focus on effective corporate communication, it turned out that Susan also had experience building women's networks. So, when I started the network at the bank, she supported me with a wealth of ideas, including the importance of opening the group to men as well as women. She gave an incredible workshop on leadership for us, helping position our initiative as an important opportunity for leadership development and cultural change. Her passion for inclusive leadership continues to inspire me to this day.

While developing our plans for the women's network, I met Kristin, a thought leader on inclusive work environments and female-leadership, and founder of WIN, the Women's International Networking organisation. Kristin has since encouraged my work at several stages of my evolution. She gave a powerful keynote speech at the opening event of the women's network at the bank, highlighting the significance of the work we had started. More recently, Kristin invited me to provide business coaching for attendees of her flagship Global Women's International Networking Conference in Rome, and to lead the entrepreneurial panel the following year in Athens. These two events were not just incredible opportunities but, since they required me to travel abroad alone, highlighted just how far I'd come along my networking journey since we had first met more than a decade before.

When I met Djamila, our intention was to exchange professional notes as our corporate roles were in the same field. We met up while I was on maternity leave, and when I told her how I was struggling with the idea of returning to work, both on a practical and emotional level, an idea came to me: "Maybe I could write freelance?" It turns out, she had a colleague who was looking for a writer. When I won that client, it was just the sign I needed that I could create my own way of working. During our first meeting when we were comparing Intranet strategies, I never imagined that one day she'd help me start my own business.

Ioanna also brought an unexpected opportunity my way. During a networking event, we connected over our common love for marketing. A couple of weeks later, over coffee, Ioanna mentioned that she'd like to start her own marketing consultancy. I shared my experiences of starting out on my own, and it was just the insights she needed to help her take the leap. A decade on, she is still successfully running her agency from her new home in London. Before she moved, she worked with the TEDx Lausanne team and, thanks to our ongoing connection, I learned of an opening within their communication team. Since I work largely alone and love TED talks, I jumped at the opportunity, and later joined their speaker team to coach thought leaders in delivering an impactful talk.

Lynda was a connection who reached out to me. When she was looking to know more about the local entrepreneurial community, her connections pointed her in my direction (thanks to my personal brand). We met over coffee more than five years ago, and since then have enjoyed many successful business collaborations and cocktail-fuelled giggles together.

As a high-performance coach and master NLP practitioner, Lynda has helped accelerate my understanding of how what we think influences what we do, and started using this knowledge to drive my success. As the mindset coach within my group business coaching program, the *Dream Clients Blueprint*, Lynda also guides my clients building a robust success mindset.

More than a decade ago, I met Sarah through LinkedIn. Over the years, our paths have weaved in and out as our businesses have grown and evolved. We've continually supported each other's journeys, shared lessons and encouragement, and appeared on each other's podcasts ... and even (now) in each other's books. Despite living in neighbouring towns, it was about seven years before we met in person! Showing that even purely digital interactions can lead to unexpected and positive outcomes.

When I met Johan, he invited me to join his new online platform for the global entrepreneurial community, Entnest. Through this platform and his personal introductions, I've met a wide array of inspiring people. Like Janene, who became my business bestie and with whom I've subsequently travelled Europe for various business and speaking engagements. James, who collaborates with myself and Janene on a monthly 'Perfecting Your Pitch' event that helps business owners better communicate their business and offers. Ida, who continually shares new ideas on how to use my experience of working with women to bring about positive change. And Bernie, who became my book mentor and publisher, a connection that made this book possible.

As you can see, many of my biggest opportunities have come about thanks to my network: starting a women's network, becoming an international public speaker and TEDx speaker coach, starting my own business, coaching women around the world, and publishing my first book. Yet, it was not evident from the start of any of these connections the extent of the opportunities they would make possible. You just never know where your next 'Hello' will take you, and that's an exciting prospect.

One thing I know, is that I would not be where I am today, if I hadn't built my VICTORY Formula, worked on my personal brand, learned the essential networking skills (on- and offline), and put these consistently into action.

The knowledge you now possess will unlock the door to many new friendships and opportunities for you too. But, as I said right back on page one, this knowledge alone won't change anything for you. You need to breathe life into your ideas and plans by allowing them to live beyond your *Networking Success Journal*, by putting them into practice, little by little, step by step, week by week, year by year.

So, grab your VICTORY Formula, conversation starters and plan, and go for it. I can't wait to hear the stories from your own networking adventures. And always remember:

You've got this!

Chapter 8

CHECKLISTS

Pre-Networking Actions

☐ Identify milestone goals

☐ Have a clear event objective

☐ Practice your compelling introduction

☐ Create your 'Would like to meet' list

☐ Prepare conversation starters

☐ Prepare conversation maintainers

☐ Prepare your brand stories

☐ Business cards, phone charger, notepad, pens

☐ Plan your outfit

☐ Update your online presence

☐ Schedule Follow up time

During the Event

☐ Smile

☐ Firm, not bone-crushing, handshake

☐ Scan for open circles

☐ Remember names (badge, 3x, association)

☐ Give your full attention

☐ Maintain good eye contact

☐ Be animated and passionate

☐ Speak for around 20% of the time

☐ Ask open questions

☐ Avoid negative conversations

☐ Share contact details (cards, LinkedIn)

☐ Use your favourite exit strategy

☐ Allow time for goodbyes

☐ Thank the organisers

Following the Event

☐ File business card and connect on LinkedIn

☐ Send thoughtful, personalised message

☐ Thank the organiser

☐ Share a social media post about the event

☐ Regularly share valuable content with new contacts, always using their name.

☐ Follow-through on any promises

☐ Arrange coffee/meetings with contacts you'd like to get to know better.

☐ Consider if any new contacts could be part of your Success Circle

☐ Stay in alignment with your personal brand

Online Networking

☐ Keep your profile up to date

☐ Share valuable advice

☐ Stay in alignment with your personal brand

☐ Have max. three core topics

☐ Have clear links to your offers, opt-ins and website

☐ Add value first

☐ Create 'open circle' content

☐ Join and participate in Groups

☐ Be consistent

☐ Use direct messages, keep them short and natural.

☐ Track your messages in a tool or spreadsheet.

☐ Move conversations off social media

☐ Try and meet in person too, don't rely solely on your online networking.

ACKNOWLEDGEMENTS

As you may have gathered from reading this book, I don't believe that success is a solo activity. So, I am hugely grateful to the numerous people who have been part of my networking journey. Some of whom you have just met. Many others will never know just how important or meaningful their friendly smile or warm welcome have been along the way.

Thank you to my book mentor and publisher Bernie Davies. Your support, insights and belief in this book have been beyond my expectations. Thank you for helping bring out a whole new side of me, not just as an author, but also in redefining what a Shy Girl is and can achieve.

Thank you to my husband and family for their unfailing support, encouragement and feedback. It means the world to me. Especially to my gorgeous daughters, thank you for understanding that Mummy needed to take some extra time to focus on writing this book, and thank you especially for all the encouragement and cwtches along the way.

And finally, to my wonderful network of Driven Female Entrepreneurs and business builders. Your community, comments and support never fail to spur me on. I look forward to where our adventures take us next.

ABOUT THE AUTHOR

Melitta Campbell is a Business and Communication Coach, helping women confidently build and grow a profitable business that enables them to live their purpose and secure the balanced lifestyle they desire.

She is also the best-selling author behind the 'Shy Girl' series of books for women in business. Starting with her advice on 'Networking for Business Success', through the series, Melitta shares how she has turned being a 'shy girl' into a quietly powerful advantage.

For more than 25 years, Melitta has been using her authentic style of communication and meaningful marketing strategies to help businesses and leaders develop respected brands and enjoy accelerated business growth. She has won prestigious awards for her innovative and engaging approach to branding.

Since 2006, she has also been using these skills to give women the tools, formulas and inspiration they need to dream bigger and achieve more in their careers and businesses.

Today, this 'shy girl' is a sought-after business coach for women, TEDx speaker coach, host of the Driven Female Entrepreneur podcast, co-founder of the 'Perfecting Your Pitch' events and membership, inspiring public speaker and international best-selling author.

Originally from Swansea in Wales, today Melitta lives in French-speaking Switzerland with her husband and two daughters, while serving her clients around the world.

You can reach out to Melitta via her website:
www.melittacampbell.com

More 'Shy Girl's Guide' books will follow soon!

Printed in Great Britain
by Amazon